Victor Discovers Treasure @ 2022 Sharon Deur

All rights reserved. No part of this publication may be reproduced or transmitted in any form or by any electronic or mechanical means including photo copying, recording, or any information storage and retrieval system now known or to be invented, without permission in writing from the publisher or the author.

Name: Deur, Sharon
Title: Victor Discovers Treasure by Sharon Deur
Series: Victor the Donkey
Illustrator/Cover Artwork: Deborah Smith
Cover Design: Robert Ousnamer

ISBN: 978-1-953114-84-6
LCCN: 2020911419
Subjects: 1. Religion/Christian Living/Devotional
2. Juvenile Nonfiction/Religious/Christian/Devotional & Prayer

Published by EA Books Publishing, a division of
Living Parables of Central Florida, Inc. a 501c3

EABooksPublishing.com

Author photo by Erin Moore, Sweet Lemon Drop Photography.

Scripture verses quoted in this book are taken from the following: The Message **(MSG)**, The International Children's Bible **(ICB)**, The New International Version **(NIV)**, The New Living Translation **(NLT)**, New King James Version **(NKJV)**, Amplified Bible **(AMP)**, Common English Bible **(CEB)**, Contemporary English Version **(CEV)**.

VICTOR DISCOVERS TREASURE

45 MORE Devotional Digs for Kids

Book 2

Victor the Donkey Series

Sharon Deur

Illustrated by Deborah Smith

 Check out Victor's Facebook page @victorthedonkey

 Website: sharondeur.com

To my Best Friend and Husband,

Dave Deur.

You enrich my journey in this life in countless ways:

always focusing on the Lord,

encouraging me every step of the way,

making me smile & laugh,

being the wisest and most patient Dad, and

by finding & sharing adventures big and little.

I love you and I thank you!

~~~~~~~~~~~~~~~~

I also dedicate this devotional to our Sons,

Kyle, Kent, and Dennis,

and to our Daughters-in-love,

Taylor and Amanda.

I am overjoyed that God chose *me* to be your Mom, by birth or marriage.

You have an incredibly special place in my heart!

You kept encouraging me and helping me to bring Victor to life.

One day we will all join dear Kent at the feet of Jesus, the Lion and The Lamb!

I love you and I thank you!

Table of Contents

He's THE Stone; You're A Stone	3	Hear That Knock At The Door?	27
A Safe Fort	4	The Only Way To Heaven	28
Not Like Victor	5	You Are THE Salt	29
Fall Into His Arms	6	An Instrument Doesn't Just Play Music	30
Give Us A Hand, Lord	7	All Of Us Are Adopted	31
Are You Smelling Sweet?	8	Better In The Shade	32
Are Your *Prayers* Smelling Sweet?	9	Hope Rope	33
Just Taste It	10	You Are The Apple Of His Eye	34
Be Hungry and Thirsty	11	Guard It	35
Bread Wonder	12	Cling Tightly	36
The Lamb of God	13	Shine Like Stars	37
Go Fishing	14	A Mirror Is Just A Mirror	38
Are you In Rough and Deep Water?	15	The Well That's Always Full	39
The Color Red	16	Creation Treasures	40
White As Snow	17	Our Lion; Our King	41
Look At Jesus	18	God's Special Rain	42
Earth Is God's Footstool	19	Wheat or Weeds?	43
How's Your Me-Power?	20	Catch Your Thoughts	44
A Strong, Safe Tower	21	Hands and Knees	45
All Kinds Of "Pots"	22	Being Like a Thirsty Deer	46
Weary, Worried, Or On Wings?	23	Are You a Victor?	47
You Are A Temple	24	Special Prayer	48
How Do People Read You?	25	Dig Deeper	49
Part Of Christ's Body	26		

Acknowledgements

I am humbled and honored to acknowldege God first! My conviction is beautifully stated by Paul in Colossians 3:17—"And whatever you do or say, do it as a representative of the Lord Jesus, giving thanks through him to God the Father." I am HIS representative! God planted the seeds for this book many years ago. *He* gave me the ideas and words! He's *my* Potter. He shapes *me* every day and He has allowed and enabled this second *book* to take shape.

He has also put precious praying and encouraging people on my path to help me:

--my loving, patient husband, Dave, who encouraged and enabled me to flex my writing "muscles."

--my *amazing* children, Kyle & Taylor; Dennis & Amanda, who inspired me, cheered me on, and helped with photography, technology, reading my first drafts, and giving physical support.

--my dear parents, Arnold & Irene Potter, and the faith foundation they gave me.

--my cheering siblings, siblings-in-love, and all of my extended family, some of whom have gone to be with Jesus already.

--my *many* faithful, gentle friends, including a *young* friend named Lukas G who inspired the idea for having Victor appear on *every* page of Book Two.

--my author-friends, Renè Schmidt and Grace Gayle, who shared their experience and discerning wisdom.

--My former neighbors, Clint and Barb McGinnis, who adore their pet donkey, Roscoe. Through photos, emails, and letters they coached me on the varied characteristics, antics, and habits of donkeys.

--the 2016-17 fourth grade class of Fremont Christian School who listened and critiqued my first rough drafts when I was substitute teaching there for two weeks.

--all the students I taught over a 24 year span. They blessed me *daily* and motivated me to keep explaining Bible truths in a way that was meaningful to *them*.

--Crystal Bowman, author of more than 100 children's books, was the first one God used to redirect my story writing to *devotional* writing. She did this during Carol Kent's Speak Up Conference in 2018. She then edited this devotional with gracious, kind honesty and expertise. Her comments inspired me and kept driving me forward.

--Cheri, Debbie, Marti, Bob, Linda, Tanya, Lily, and the *entire* EA Publishing team were godly "coaches"--patient with me and thorough in their explanations. They were always just an email or a phone call away. *Debbie truly depicted each biblical metaphor with excellence.*

--My cousin Gloria E who designed my website with distinction.

To *all* of you mentioned above, I thank you and I thank God *for* you! "May you be richly rewarded by the Lord…under whose wings you have come to take refuge" (Ruth 2:12).

Introduction

More Treasure. More Adventure. More gold. Let's keep hunting for it!

In this second book, Victor the donkey is going to help us dig up MORE *word treasures* that God put in *His* Book, the Bible. These are words that put a *picture* in our minds so we can remember and understand God's promises and how to live our lives for Him!

Sometimes our parents and grandparents speak in *word treasures*:

"The ball was flat as a pancake" means there is no air in it.

"I've got butterflies in my stomach," means I'm very nervous.

"Busy as a bee" means working extra hard to get a lot of things done.

This book is meant to be a map; a guide—to discover and explore Bible treasures like these:
God calls you and me a temple, a stone, salt, a living letter. *He* is called Bread, a Lion, a Lamb.

God wants to get us thinking about Him and live in ways that put a big smile on His face! Our reward—the "gold"—after all the treasure digging, is living on earth *trusting* in a Jesus we cannot see *and* someday living in Heaven *with* Jesus looking at Him face to face!

See if you can spot Victor the donkey on *every* page! He is so excited to help you dig into the Bible! "Victor" is a *pretend* name for a *real* animal that we read about more than 100 times in the Bible! One time—are you ready for this?—a donkey talked (check out Book One and Numbers 22:21-39)! Oh, God is *full* of surprises! I can't wait to tell you more!

The Bible says in Isaiah 45:3, "I'll lead you to buried treasures . . . " Thanks for "digging" with me!

Note to Parents & Grandparents: In Romans 6, Paul describes our new lives in Christ as *freedom* from being slaves of sin and serving a *new* Master. Then in verse 19 (from THE MESSAGE) Paul says, "I'm using this freedom language because it's easy to picture." Jesus told parables to help His followers understand kingdom concepts more clearly. THAT is the purpose of this devotional: making the language of the Bible and following Jesus "easy to picture!" I know you share in my heart's desire to help your children understand the gospel message *and* Jesus' Kingdom metaphors so that they are drawn into a tighter relationship with Him!

When you see ⛏ it refers to the Bible passage(s) that supports that particular devotional. It's the "*Dig Deeper Bible Truth*" (somehow *shovels* and *treasure* are just meant to be together). In the back of this devotional all the Dig Deeper Bible Truths are written out. The versions used were prayerfully selected according to what young children can understand most easily. The 🐴 indicates an *action*/activity the children are encouraged to do to give practical application to the truth explained.

MEET JESUS

- A Miracle Baby; A Miracle-Worker!
- Son of God-- The God Who made this world and **you**!
- Invisible, but oh so Real!
- Made Blind people see!
- Loves us sooooo much that He died on a cross for us!
- Our Best Friend Forever (BFF) He's crazy about you!
- Made lame people walk!
- He Walked on Water!
- Full of Kindness!
- Lived on Earth for a while, **now** in Heaven **and** in hearts! ♡ Yup! He's King of the Universe, but chooses to live in **our** hearts! ♡ AMAZING!
- Our Leader through life!
- Heart Changer! Heart Filler!
- Best and <u>Only</u> Eraser of our sins!

MEET VICTOR

- Dependable!
- Smart!
- Calm!
- Strong!
- Friendly!
- Guards Sheep!
- Sure-footed!

He's THE Stone; You're A Stone

There is not really much difference between a stone and a rock. Victor knows that! Both are hard. Both can be very big or very small. In the Bible there is no difference either. It says *God* is like a Rock, 🪏 A but it also says *Jesus* is *like* a Living Stone!

🪏 B (God, Jesus, and the Holy Spirit are the same!)

In the Bible, a very good man named Peter says that when the bad people put Jesus on a cross, it was like throwing a stone away! 😢

We are made in God's image. That means we are *like* Him—kind and loving to others. But of course we are not *perfect* like *God* is! So Peter says we are **like** *living stones* being built into a home for God—a place where God WANTS to live! 🪏 B
Jesus is perfect. We are not. He wants to live in us anyway and make us something very special. *YAHOO!*

Treasure Talk: Jesus is like a Living Stone. We are like little ones.

A 1 Sam. 2:2
B 1 Pet. 2:4-5

Find about 5 or 6 small stones. With glue stick them on top of each other. Pray: "Jesus, please help me be a living stone, always pointing to you! And thank You for always being MY Living Stone!"

A Safe Fort

Snow forts. Tree forts. Sofa cushion forts. Table forts. These are all fun to make.

Fun forts act like a *fence* to keep us cozy and protected from wondering and wandering little brothers or sisters. We have a safe place to pretend, to play, to read, or to sleep.

GOD is a safe place! A,B,C

This is a *promise* and a rich *treasure*! He may be invisible, but He is oh, so real and the BEST Listener ever! Cozy up to Him (in your fort or out).

Pretend you're in His lap.

Talk to Him as if you see Him 'cause He sure sees YOU! D

Treasure Talk: You can cozy up to God anytime, anywhere. He is safe.

DIG DEEPER

A Ps. 32:7
B Ps. 62:8
C Ps. 18:2
D Gen. 16:13

With permission, make some kind of fort! Pray to the God Who sees you! If you're with someone else you can pray together!

Not Like Victor

We can learn so much from donkey habits in this book, *but* when we dig deep into God's words for us, it tells us **not** to be like a horse or a donkey. **A** Let's find out why.

On a farm, horses and donkeys need people leading and guiding them with ropes or reins. Those things hold them back or lead them ahead.

God gave animals and people their brains, but they work very differently. Animals cannot *think* like people do. They can't *understand* like people can. OUR brains are made to understand!

We understand that God's Holy Spirit leads us and guide us. It's almost as if He whispers to our brains to **do** or **not do** something.

If we ask God to make us wise, He will! **B** Animals can't do that.

Treasure Talk: We like Victor, but God made us VERY different from him.

DIG DEEPER
A Ps. 32:9
B Ps. 32:8

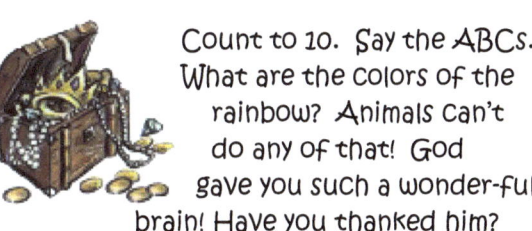

Count to 10. Say the ABCs. What are the colors of the rainbow? Animals can't do any of that! God gave you such a wonder-full brain! Have you thanked him?

Falling Into His Arms

Think a minute about different safety nets: a fishing net will keep the wiggly fish you just caught from getting away. And it keeps you safe from a fish tail slapping you in the face! At the circus, there are nets to catch someone who might slip and fall. Hard-hat workers helping to build tall buildings need to know that if they take a wrong step a net will catch them. Firemen use nets to catch people or pets jumping from a burning building. Trampoline nets keep us from tumbling to the ground.

Safety nets in the Bible are God's arms!  **A** No, not REAL arms. It's treasure talk for "Hey, God will protect you from danger! God will protect you from Satan! Just ask! Just trust!

Workers or circus people have to trust and not be afraid. They *know* that if they fall, the nets will catch them! What are you afraid of? What are you worried about?

Are you believing—**trusting**—that God has you in His arms? In His safety net? **B**

Treasure Talk: God is safer than a strong net.

 **A** Deut. 33:27
B Ps. 56:3-4

Fall backwards into the arms of a grown-up who loves you very much! Do it with your eyes closed! You TRUSTED them, didn't you? That is like the invisible arms of our Great God!

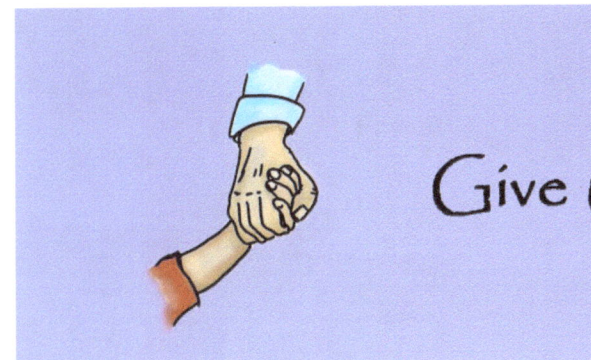

Give Us A Hand, Lord

Moses was an important leader in the Bible. He led millions of God's people, Israel, out of the country where they were slaves for over 200 years! God said, "That's enough! Moses, I will help you free my people and get them to a safe land."

But when they left they had to cross a VERY BIG sea! The people were afraid (donkeys like Victor are afraid, too, when they sense danger is near).

The bad king and his army of that old country were chasing God's people! Where would they go? There was only water in front of them. *God told Moses to stretch out his hand*.

He did! THEN the water split in half! In between was dry ground! It was like a *road* for them to get to the other side. By the time the bad army got to the sea, the water was back to its normal deep, deep self. So sad for the bad army.

[Stop reading right now and go to "Dig Deeper" 🪣 A to read the story in God's Words!]

In Psalm 136 we read, "His love never quits" 26 times! It also says God took Israel's hand in His powerful Hand." And you just read that He told Moses to stretch out <u>his</u> hand!

He was giving Moses a treasure about HANDS!

Hands are for helping! Ever heard someone say, "I'll give you a hand?"

God is being His amazing Self and putting a picture in our minds of how MUCH He loves us and how MUCH He will help us if we ask Him!

Treasure Talk: God will give us a Hand if we just ask. His love never quits! B

A Ex. 14
B Ps. 136:4,12-14

 Put your hand in the hand of whoever is reading with you right now. Pray: "Jesus, thank You for always holding My hand! I need it!"

Are You Smelling Sweet?

Here's an interesting fact that Victor wants you to know: he and his donkey relatives don't stink! You can pet them or cuddle them, and your dog at home will never know!

You don't "stink" either because you take baths or showers, but our treasure talk today is about having a GOOD "smell." As Jesus-believers and Jesus-lovers, God wants our **words** and our **actions** to give off a "sweet smell" and make other kids want a "taste" of Him too!

Real sweet smells for people like us are fresh-baked chocolate chip cookies, hot pizza, pie, or a roasting turkey. Those sweet smells make us want a *taste* of whatever it is that's tickling our noses! This treasure is in food language because we *all* have to eat (even Victor can sniff out good food). We love foods that look good or smell good.

Some people we meet already love Jesus. Some don't even *know* Him. Are you a "sweet smell" to both?

Treasure Talk: Be a Christian that others want to be with.

DIG DEEPER   2 Cor. 2:15

Go find something in the fridge that you like the smell of! Are YOU someone who people like to be with because you love Jesus and show it?

Are Your Prayers Smelling Sweet?

Now you know WE can be a sweet smell to others, but the Bible also says our PRAYERS are a sweet smell to God!

Smoke rises from a campfire. Steam rises from boiling water on the stove.

Treasure talk says that's like our prayers rising to God. A

He loves to hear from us!

He treasures us, remember? B When you *treasure* someone you want them to talk with you. God wants to hear from you. Tell God what is on your mind and in your heart HE IS SAFE!

It is *VERY SPECIAL* to God when He hears from His children!

Treasure Talk: Your talks to God are like a sweet smell to Him.

DIG DEEPER
A Psalm 141:2
B Deut. 7:6

With permission light a candle. Blow it out! Watch the smoke. Soon it disappears. That's like your prayers rising to God. He hears them, tucks them away in His Heart, and answers them just right!

Just Taste It

God gave us (and Victor) *noses* to smell things and *tongues* to taste with. Since it's God Who made us and the animals, He uses "smell" and "taste" to help us understand His Bible and to get us ready for His heaven.

Did your mom or dad ever put something new on your plate and say, "Just give it a taste; you may like it?" Then you tried it and WOW! They were right. You liked it and you gobbled it up.

The Bible's tasty treasure talk here is: *just try* loving God, *just try* praying to Him; *just try* obeying His words. **You'll find out how good God is!** A

With *real* food, if we love the taste of something we could eat too much too fast and get a huge tummy ache! But we don't have to worry about that when we taste God's words or His kindness; His goodness or His love. God WANTS us to keep "tasting" and "eating" them up! B.

David, that caring shepherd who wrote so many songs about God, said, "Your word is so pleasing to my taste buds—it's sweeter than honey in my mouth!" C

Treasure Talk: Just take a "taste" of God; you'll love Him!

DIG DEEPER

A Ps. 34:8
B 1 Pet. 2:2-3
C Ps. 119:103

The next time your family sits down for a meal together, make a little sign for everyone's plate. On each one write: "Open your mouth and taste how good God is."

Be Hungry and Thirsty

"I'm hungry!" I'm thirsty!" Ever said those words? When you say you are hungry and thirsty, you are thinking about REAL food or REAL water, milk, or juice. After you eat a good meal, you are full for a while, but a few hours later you may be hungry again.

Jesus said that He is happy if we are hungry and thirsty *for God!* A

That's treasure talk for simply *wanting* to *love* Him, trust Him, and serve Him! We can never get too full of God's love, so it's always good to want more of Him. We have to help other people want that too!

What if you tasted a new kind of food and said, "Yuck! That's terrible!" Do you think your friends would want a taste? NO! But if you said, "That's the best food I've ever had!" Well, just watch your friends beg you for a bite! B

If you've had a "taste" of God—if you love Him, pray to Him, and call yourself a Christian, *then share Him!* Make your friends hungry and thirsty for the God who can take *them* to Heaven too some day!

Treasure Talk: Be hungry and thirsty for God and make loving God tasty to others!

A Mt. 5:6
B Ps. 63:1

Next time you hear yourself say, "That's delicious!" then whisper, "Jesus, You're delicious too!"

Bread Wonder

Before reading, go to "Dig Deeper" in the back. Read 🪏A about the incredible wonder Jesus did when he took a young boy's lunch and made it GROW bigger to feed over 5,000 people! AMAZING! [Fun note: Victor eats plants—not bread, not fish.]

Soon after this bread wonder happened, Jesus shared a treasure talk with His friends: He said," God's bread is the One [a Person!] who comes down from heaven and gives life to the world." 🪏B He was talking about JESUS! Jesus came to earth, did tons of wonders, died on a cross, came back to life, and wants us to believe ALL of it. THEN we get life in Heaven someday—life that lasts forever! Now THAT's the BEST wonder in the world! Jesus said clearly, "I am the *Bread* that gives life." 🪏C

If bread stays out of its wrapper too long, it will get dry, crusty, and moldy. Not only was Jesus a Bread *Wonder*, He was also a Bread *Expert*. He knew that people who read His words would think about *real* bread, so He made it very clear that *nothing* in Heaven spoils! 🪏D

Treasure Talk: Bread is good for you but *Jesus* is THE Bread that gives eternal life!

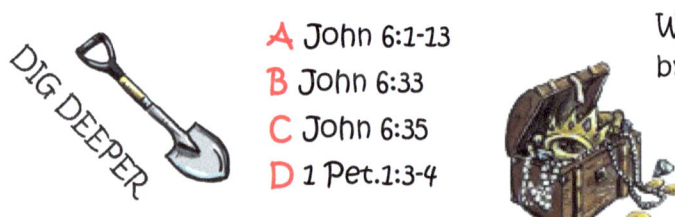

DIG DEEPER
A John 6:1-13
B John 6:33
C John 6:35
D 1 Pet.1:3-4

With permission leave a slice of bread out on the counter for 2 weeks. Watch it get older and more yucky. Say this prayer: "Jesus, thank you for being my Fresh Bread of eternal life!"

The Lamb of God

When we give up something we love because something else is more important, it is called a **săc-ri-fīce**! We sacrifice a favorite *toy* at Christmas because someone with no toys needs it more. We sacrifice TV for homework. We sacrifice our *time* so that we can do a job for someone who needs our help.

When Jesus came to earth to die for our sin, God gave up—*sacrificed*—His only Son to die on a cross so that we could live in His heaven some day!   **A** That is **THE BIGGEST** sacrifice OF ALL!

So what did people do about their sins before Jesus was born?
They had to sacrifice something special to them to show that they were sorry for sinning. That special something was often a little *lamb* that belonged to the family. It was hard for them to do, but they wanted God to forgive their sins, so they did it.

Lambs are *very* special in God's Bible. God took the lamb idea and used it in His treasure talk to call Jesus the *Lamb* of God Who takes away the sins of the world!   **B**

Thank You, God!

Treasure Talk: Jesus IS the Lamb of God.

   **A** John 3:16
B John 1:29

 Make a *sacrifice* today for someone. When they ask you why you did that nice thing, say, "'Cause God made a bigger One for me! I love you!"

Go Fishing

Victor's tummy cannot stand fish, but ours can! Many of us love to go fishing with our poles, line, and bait. Jesus and His friends loved it too, but they only used nets.

One night Jesus asked His friends to load up their two boats and go out fishing with Him. They had been fishing all evening since supper. It was their job. So when Jesus asked them to go out again, they said, "But Lord, we've been fishing all evening and didn't catch a thing! But because You say so, we will do it again." They listened. They obeyed.

They caught so many fish that each of their boats began to sink! That's a LOT of fish! A

Then Jesus said, "From now on you will be fishing for people." B That means Jesus wanted them to *tell* others about Him so they would believe and go to His heaven someday. He wants us to do that—"Tell people about me," He says. "Don't be afraid! I'll always be with you." C If God can make a *donkey* talk, He will for sure give us the right words to say!

Treasure Talk: Listen and obey Jesus—go tell people about Him.

DIG DEEPER
A Luke 5:4-8
B Luke 5:10
C Mt.28:18-20

Make a list of people you know that don't know Jesus. Draw a fishing pole on top of that list and write: "I'M GOING FISHING!"

Are You In Rough and Deep Water?

Jesus loved being in a fishing boat with His friends. He loved the water. Jesus also knew that a *storm* could come up suddenly and make His boat rock and roll because of strong winds!

Since Jesus is God, He had the power to tell storms to stop! A

Since Jesus is God, He could walk on *top* of water and help His friend Peter do the same thing! B

Rough and deep water is like troubles, pain, and problems that we have. But the *treasure* is that God goes **with** us and **helps** us with troubles, pain, and problems. C They don't *always* go away, but at least God is hanging on to us and reaches out a hand to us just like He did for Peter. D

Treasure Talk: Jesus WILL help with our problems. Just ask Him.

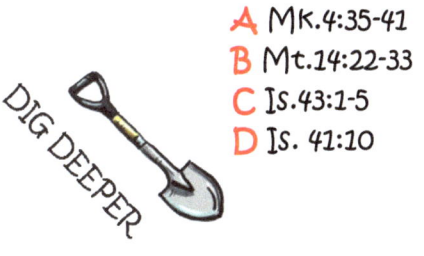

A Mk. 4:35-41
B Mt. 14:22-33
C Is. 43:1-5
D Is. 41:10

Next time you're in the bathtub, put a little plastic toy person in a small boat. Keeping the water inside the tub, make some waves until the toy falls out. Put it back in. Let the water go quiet and say, "Thank You, Jesus, for helping **me** in rough waters!"

The Color Red

If Victor were to be injured or cut, he would cry almost like you, but you probably won't see any tears. That is how God created him.

If *you* cut your finger or scrap your knee, it hurts. It bleeds. You may cry.

When Jesus died on a cross in order to erase our sins, it hurt. He bled. He probably cried.

Blood is red. So when "red" shows up in the Bible it is treasure talk for either *sin* or the *blood* that Jesus shed to save us from our sins. 🪣A

Here are two stories from the Bible that help us understand:

#1 When Miss Rahab put a *red rope* out her window to save her and her family, it was a hint that Jesus saves us from our sins. 🪣B

#2 A lamb's blood painted on a door post saved *God's* people from some very bad people. Remember when we talked about Jesus being called the Lamb of God? 🪣C

Treasure Talk: Jesus' red blood reminds us that He erased (forgives) our sins.

A Is. 1:18
B Josh. 2:17–19
C Ex. 12:7, 13

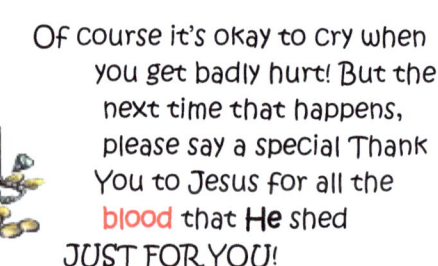

Of course it's okay to cry when you get badly hurt! But the next time that happens, please say a special Thank You to Jesus for all the blood that He shed JUST FOR YOU!

White As Snow

Maybe you live in an area where you get snow in the winter. After a fresh fall of this fluffy white stuff, it is beautiful! It's like God threw a pure white blanket onto the earth to cover up the left over shriveled red leaves and brownish grass.

The Bible says that our sins are bright red 🪣**A,** but that *same* verse says they *can be* as white as snow! They *can* be! How do we to make that happen?

We *believe* that Jesus died on the cross for our sins! *

If you get a **red** stain on a **white** shirt, you're very happy if Mom is able get it out. Jesus knows that, so He compares *sin* to a *stain*. If you make the *choice* to believe that Jesus died to make your heart white as snow, the angels in heaven have a party for you! 🪣**B** Picture that! An angel party JUST FOR YOU!

"White" is such a treasure-word to God! His throne in Heaven is even white! 🪣**C**

Treasure Talk: Our hearts are white like snow if we let Jesus in!

DIG DEEPER

A Is. 1:18
B Lk. 15:10
C Rev. 20:11

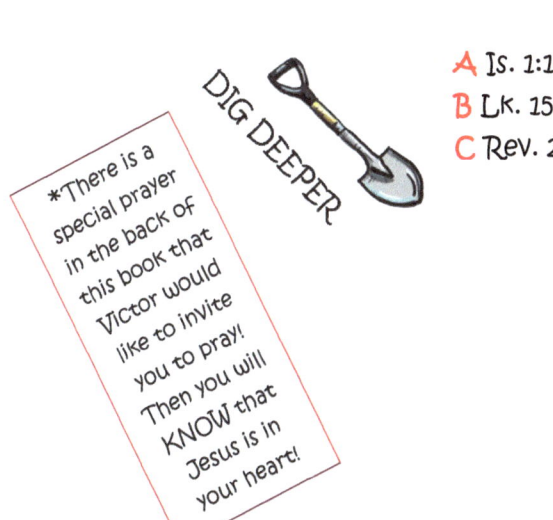

With permission AND help, wear some old clothes and scribble on a white cotton rag with a red washable marker (that red is like our sins). Now ask the adult to help you dip that rag into a bleach/water mixture. Watch the red disappear! *Thank JESUS for making your heart white like snow!*

*There is a special prayer in the back of this book that Victor would like to invite you to pray! Then you will KNOW that Jesus is in your heart!

Look At Jesus

Victor is often found on a farm. He loves watching seeds go into the ground. When a farmer is planting a corn field, Victor notices that the farmer's eyes stare from his tractor to a spot straight ahead. Sometimes it is a tree or a bush on the far side of the field. When the farmer does this, his tractor will go *straight*. If his eyes *leave* that spot, he will have a crooked corn row. [Victor *does* know that many farmers and ranchers have tractors that do this automatically now. It's called GPS—<u>G</u>lobal <u>P</u>ositioning <u>S</u>ystem.]

The Bible's treasure today tells us that we must keep our eyes on Jesus! Hey! A new GPS: **<u>God's</u> <u>P</u>ositioning <u>S</u>ystem!**

How do we keep our eyes on Him if He is invisible? We talk to Him in prayer. We *think* about Him and what He did for us on the cross. We *listen* to or read the Bible to learn more about Him.

Jesus had to keep His eyes on God while He was on that wooden cross. He kept thinking, "I'm hurting right now because my Father God loves me and He loves every child and grown-up on earth. I'm hurting so they may go the Father God someday. I'm paying for *their* sins and I am happy to do it!" Let's have a personal praise party *every* day thanking Jesus for keeping His eyes on the Father!

Treasure Talk: Keep thinking and learning about Jesus!

Heb. 12:2

Go into your yard with a friend or a parent. Stand at one end and stare at a faraway tree, bush, or post. Walk toward it without looking at your feet. Ask the person with you how straight your path was. Now try it by just looking at your feet. What's the difference? *"Fix your eyes on Jesus!"*

Earth Is God's Footstool

Victor usually sleeps standing up. When *you* are tired, it feels good to plop into a big comfy chair that has a footrest. You might even fall asleep.

The dentist's chair has a footrest, too, but it is hard to fall asleep there!

In the Bible God says, "Heaven is my throne; earth is my footstool." 🪏 A

God knew that people had seen a king's *throne* before. Since it usually had a very high seat, it always had a *footrest* for the king's feet—to keep them from dangling loose.

A footstool (or footrest) was put in the exact place where the king wanted it. He owned it. He controlled it.

That's like this earth God made! He owns it. He controls it. 🪏 **B He's King!**

Treasure Talk: God is the King Who rules the whole earth!

 A Mt. 5:34,35
B Ps. 24:1

Try sitting on a chair where your legs and feet just hang. Now add a footstool. Ahhh, feel better? God feels better when we let *Him* be in control. Ask Him to help you with EVERYTHING!

How's Your Me-Power?

We learned that we are like trees and our "fruit" is how we act. One of those actions is called *self-control.* If we get angry quickly or shout and pout because something is not going our way, then we don't have much control over ourselves—no *me-power!*

Satan likes that, but God is *very* sad.

If a house has its windows or doors missing and there are just holes there instead, someone could come in and take whatever they wanted. The Bible says *we* are like that house if we can't control our anger. 🪣**A** Satan easily creeps in. Satan is like a robber or a roaring lion that comes into our heart and tries to make us do and say things that God doesn't want us to do and say. 🪣**B**

But by asking God to help us with our anger, we will win over Satan! 🪣**C YAHOO!**
Then our hearts become burglar proof!

Treasure Talk: The only one who is able to control your anger is you—WITH GOD-POWER!

A Prov. 25:28
B 1 Pet. 5:8
C Ps. 60:10-12

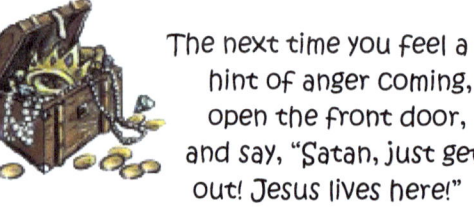

The next time you feel a hint of anger coming, open the front door, and say, "Satan, just get out! Jesus lives here!"

A Strong, Safe Tower

There are many ways to help Victor have fun! Give him an empty bucket with a treat inside. Give him a large rubber ball. Even orange safety cones make Victor giggle (okay—*bray*) with delight.

You may have played "Tag" with your friends or family! One person who's "It" closes their eyes and counts to 20 while everyone else goes to hide. "It" runs to find the others. BUT if those hiding are speedy, they can run to a special safe spot and escape from getting tagged.

The Bible calls Jesus our "safe tower." That means He is our "safe spot." **A**

Who or *what* are we running from in this life? ➔Satan, sadness, feeling lonely, danger, or *anything* that makes us worried.

How do we run to Jesus? ➔Just say His name! THAT name, "Jesus," scares Satan silly and *he* runs! Jesus' name gives us a quiet feeling; a place of peace and calm that is hard to put into words. He is **safe!** Jesus understands! **B, C**

Treasure Talk: Jesus is *always* our safety spot!

A Prov. 18:10
B Ps. 27:5
C Joel 2:32

DIG DEEPER

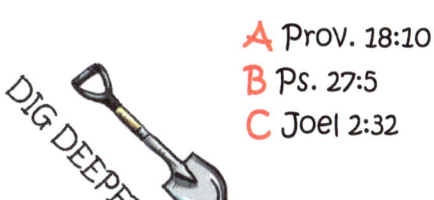

Find at least 3 friends or family members and play a game of Tag! Then talk how about Jesus is your "Safe Place;" your Strong Tower!

All Kinds of "Pots"

Cooking pots can be electric, stove-top, or made for a camp fire. They can be big or small; black, red, or silver. But they *all* can be filled with some tasty food!

Flower pots may be colorful or plain; breakable or plastic; indoor or outdoor, big or small. But they all hold beautiful flowers or plants!

When we taste the food or enjoy the flowers, the look of the pot doesn't even matter. It's what's *inside* that counts!

We have learned that the Bible says we are like clay pots. God shaped us just right from the beginning and keeps on shaping us every day. For us, as God's children, it is also what's inside that counts!

The Bible's treasure talk says that God pours into us—His special pot—some VERY IMPORTANT NEWS! News that Jesus is our King! That Jesus died for our sins! That Jesus rose from the dead and is in Heaven making a place for us! That news is a *treasure!*

If we have *that* treasure inside of us, and if we do our BEST to "pour it out" to other people, then what we look like on the outside DOES NOT MATTER AT ALL!

Treasure Talk: It does NOT matter whether you are short or tall; red, yellow, black, or white; poor or rich; good in math or not-so-good . . . all that matters is what is inside your heart and whether you believe that God is King!

DIG DEEPER 2 Cor. 4:6-7

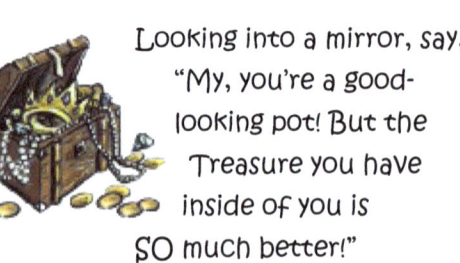

Looking into a mirror, say, "My, you're a good-looking pot! But the Treasure you have inside of you is SO much better!"

Weary, Worried, Or On Wings?

When Victor is weary, he's just plain tired. For people "weary" can mean tired, worried, afraid, sick, sad, or mad. If you are feeling *any* of those, then there is GREAT news for you: if you pray and ask God to help you with *any* or *all* of those feelings, you will feel as though you just took off on the wings of an eagle! A

Eagles' wings are big, strong, and powerful. Eagles can fly as high as mountains! If grown-ups or kids see an eagle, they talk about it for weeks! It's an eye-prize! A gift!
The *treasure* in God's Book says *He* is like that strong, powerful eagle! He makes us strong. He helps us when we are weary.

Our job is to be patient and never give up hope, trust, or believing in what He can do! B

Treasure Talk: God promises to change your feelings and thoughts for the better if you *know* and *believe* HE is in control.

A Is. 40:28-31
B Ps. 27:14

Ask someone to help you make a simple paper airplane. Draw some eyes and feathers on it. Glue a couple cotton balls on it (those are your troubles!). Fly it! Say, "Thank You, God, for taking care of all my "weary stuff"!

You Are A Temple

In Bible times people worshipped God in a building they called a *temple*. God asked them to build it. But when God sent Jesus to this earth, four things happened that changed EVERYTHING:

#1 Jesus died on a cross to save us from our sins.
#2 Jesus became alive again!
#3 God gave Jesus His Holy Spirit.
#4 Jesus gave God's Holy Spirit to us! A

Read that again. Those four sentences tell us what the whole Bible is about!

Since Jesus gave the Holy Spirit to live IN us, it was God Who said, "Okay, people, we don't need a temple anymore B—YOU are God's temple! C **My Sprit lives in YOU!** Is the light on? Can other people tell that My Spirit lives inside you? How are you treating my 'temple'? Are you eating healthy? Are you making GOOD plans in your heart? Is your mind thinking of Me more than anything else?"

Treasure Talk: God's Holy Spirit lives in YOU!
[If you love God the Father, then you love Jesus, His Son. The Holy Spirit is the part of God that He gave to live inside you! It's a little bit like an apple core, the seeds, and the part you eat—it's all part of the same apple! The Father, the Son and The Holy Spirit are all God! Hard to understand, isn't it? And that's okay! It's a mysterious Treasure that we don't HAVE to understand! We just have to believe it!]

A Acts 2:32-33
B Acts 17:24
C 1 Cor. 3:16

With an adult's help cut an apple in half. Take out just the black seeds. Put them in a small bowl where you can see them EVERY day. Those little black seeds will give life to a new apple tree. God's Holy Spirit gives new life in a different sort of way . . . the way that leads you to Heaven!

How Do People Read You?

It is fun to get a letter in the mail! It has *your* name on it. Someone must have cared enough about you to take the time to write. You can read it as often as you like and it makes you happy.

The Bible's treasure talk says that we are like a walking letter. 🪏 A People *read* us! That sounds funny, but other people know a lot about us just by watching us and listening to us talk. What do *you*, as a letter, look like and sound like? 🪏 B, C

> Does your face look happy or grumpy?
> How do people in a store hear you talking to your parents?
> Do you share or are you selfish with your toys?
> Do you act kindly to older people and people with special needs?
> Are you slow to get angry or do you get angry quickly?

If loving Jesus is the best part of your life, then your "letter-writing" will be easy!

Treasure Talk: Your kind, good actions and words are God's show 'n tell in front of others.

DIG DEEPER
A 2 Cor. 3:3
B Prov. 20:11
C Eph. 4:29

Go on your knees right now and ask God for His help in being a "letter" people WANT to see and hear. Add this: "God, help me be Your 'show 'n tell.' In Jesus Name, Amen."

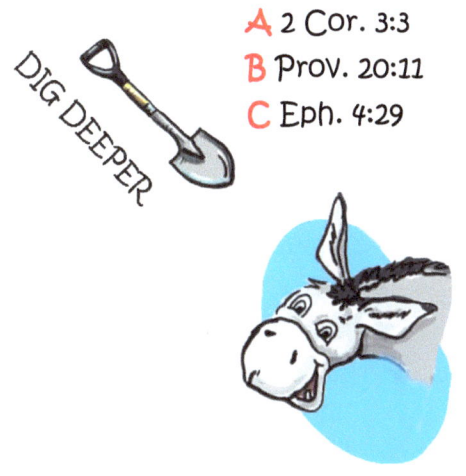

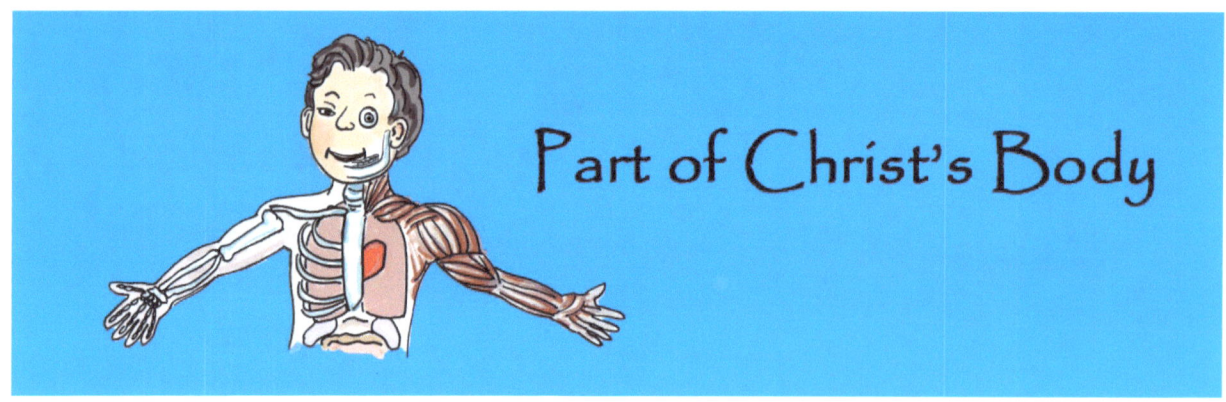

Part of Christ's Body

Victor has about 205 bones and over 700 muscles. We have 206 bones and over 600 muscles. God planned and formed all of His creatures just right!

Hearts and lungs pump blood and air to all parts of the body. Stomachs mix and mash food and make sure it gets sent to the right places for energy. God put our bodies together *just* as He wanted and He put our heads on top! The heart, lungs, stomach, muscles, and bones have *jobs* to do. Each part of the body is different, but each one is *super* important. They cannot work alone!

Today's Bible treasure tells us that ALL people who believe and love Jesus are called His Body.

🔨 **A** HE is the head! 🔨 **B** Each person is a member of Christ's body and each has something important to do.

In Christ's "body" we all have different jobs to do too. We need each other. We help each other. We cannot all be good at the same thing! Body parts are different. Christ's body parts—*people*—are all different too.

Treasure Talk: All parts of our bodies have a job. People have work to do as part of Christ's body.

DIG DEEPER
A 1 Cor. 12:27
B Col. 1:18

Talk with Mom or Dad about the jobs people have in church. How are they different? How can you thank them for doing their jobs so well! Now talk about what YOU are good at in the body of Christ!

Hear That Knock At The Door?

If someone comes knocking at the door of your house, Mom or Dad will answer it. If they know the person well, they might say, "So good to see you! Come in and eat with us!" In the very last book of the Bible, God puts a picture in our minds of *Himself* knocking at the "door" of our hearts. **A**

We have a *real* heart inside of us that pumps blood throughout our bodies and we have a treasure talk heart where we say God *lives*. If God lives in us, we are different! We love Him back, we obey Him, we obey our parents, and we believe in Jesus, God's Son.

God wants this so much that He will keep trying and trying! Treasure talk says He will gently knock and knock until that person "opens the door!" It is a *choice* whether to open it or not. It is a *choice* whether to believe in God or not. But if we do—if we say, "Yes, God, come into my heart and life. Change me forever," then He will be our best Friend—all the way to Heaven. It's like your best friend eating with you *all* the time.

Treasure Talk: Have you opened the door of your heart to let Jesus in? He only knocks because He loves you so much! **B**

A Rev. 3:20
B John 3:16

Ask an adult you love to stand outside the door to your house. Ask them to knock gently a few times. Open it and say, "I opened the real door for you, and I'm opening the door of my *heart* to God!"

Kids, if you want to ask Jesus (God's Son!) to come into your heart right now, there is a special prayer in the back of the book just for you! This will be THE MOST important choice of your life!

The Only Way To Heaven

Donkeys like Victor are masters at walking narrow (skinny) pathways. They take small steps. They put their back feet in exactly the same spot where their front feet were. And they can do this while carrying a very heavy pack. Donkeys aren't scared easily, and if they ARE scared they just stop and don't go ahead anymore. They move when they know it is safe.

Jesus tells us that the way to heaven is a like a *narrow* road, not wide! 🪏A

That treasure talk means there is ONLY **ONE** WAY to get to heaven and that is by believing in Jesus Christ!

The "wide road" means people think they have *lots* of ways they can get into God's heaven— "I just have to do good things for others!" "I can't use bad words." "I must always obey Mom, Dad and teachers." They keep making *lists* of things to do or not do.

Even though ALL of those things ARE *very* important, Dos and Don'ts will not get you to heaven. *Only Jesus can do that!* He said it Himself: "I am the Road . . . No one gets to the Father apart from me." 🪏B

Now is that road always easy to travel? **No!** Jesus has the answer for that too: "In this world you will have trouble. But be brave! I have defeated the world!" 🪏C

Treasure Talk: Believing in Jesus is the ONLY way to get into His heaven (the prayer in the back of this book will help you do that!).

A Mt. 7:13-14
B Jn. 14:6
C Jn. 16:33

Take some "baby steps" across the kitchen floor to the other side (heel-to-toe). Just like Victor, this may not be easy, but it gets you there! Pray: "Jesus, thank you for helping me get to heaven just by believing in You—even though the way may not always be easy!"

You Are THE Salt!

People like you and animals like Victor need to have salt! It adds vitamins and flavor to food. If it was missing, you would know it!

Today salt lasts a very long time in our cupboards. When Jesus was on earth salt added taste to food too, but their kind of salt could *lose* its flavor. People would just throw it out on the dirt street for Victor and his friends to trample on.

Jesus tells us that we are the salt of the earth. **A**
We are on this earth to make Jesus flavor-full!

If we are full of joy, full of kindness, full of thanks because Jesus lives in our hearts, *THEN we are being like salt!* Other people will want a "taste" of Jesus! They will want to know Him, too!

But what if we are *not* joyful, kind, or thankful? Well, that is Bible treasure talk for *losing* saltiness. Jesus cannot use unsalted people. **B**

Treasure Talk: Be the kind of person that makes Jesus sound Oh, so good! Be "salt" that Jesus can use!

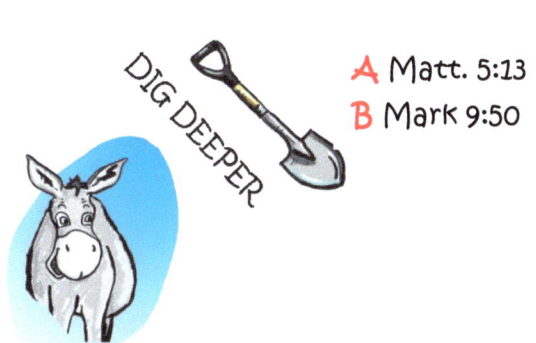

DIG DEEPER
A Matt. 5:13
B Mark 9:50

Ask Mom if she would prepare two simple dishes of the same food that you like. Ask her to salt one the way you like it and leave the other one unsalted. With a blindfold on, taste-test each. Salt makes a difference—do you agree? Ask God to make you a salty Christian!

An Instrument Doesn't Just Play Music

Do you know anyone who plays the piano, flute, violin, cello, trumpet, or trombone? They practice. They enjoy it. They take good care of their instrument. They play it to give joy to others. Even your own singing voice can be an instrument! Music is one of God's gifts to us! It can even calm Victor if it is played quietly.

God loves music! The Bible talks about music in *hundreds* of different ways. So it is not a surprise that He wants US to be HIS instruments. He wants us to speak up about Him; to tell other people what He has done for us.

THAT is music to His ears! THAT makes Him so very happy!

If you want to play an instrument for the school band, you get to *choose* which one you'd like to try. The Bible's treasure says that God *chooses us* to be His instruments!

He thinks we are *that* special! Shout **"YAHOO!"** right now!

Treasure Talk: You are God's chosen instrument! Make some incredible, beautiful "music" for Him!

DIG DEEPER 1 Pet. 2:9-10   Make up your own song thanking God for choosing you as HIS instrument!

All Of Us Are Adopted

If you've been "adopted" into your family by Dad and Mom, welcome to the club!

God is our *heavenly* Father and His Treasure Map clearly says if we are believers, we've been adopted as *His* children! 🪏A   Every single one of us who loves Jesus is in the Adoption Club! [This is when you can bray like Victor—it means YAHOO!]

A SUPER COOL fact is that there are *four* people in the Bible who were also adopted on this earth:

#1—**Moses** was adopted by a queen. When he grew up he became a leader to take God's people out of slavery!

#2—**Esther** was adopted by her older cousin. She grew up and became a queen who set her family and friends free from some bad people.

#3—**JESUS** Himself was adopted by His dad on earth--Joseph! Jesus grew up to save ALL OF US from our sins! *He changed the whole world!*

#4—**YOU**--"All who are led by God's Spirit are God's sons and daughters." 🪏B

THIS should make us jump-up-and-down-happy! Go ahead do that right now!

Treasure Talk: We are <u>all</u> adopted by God! He is our Father Who loves us more than we could *ever* imagine!

A Eph. 1:5
B Rom. 8:14-17

Make & decorate a very cool sign that says:
**God has adopted me!
I am His child!**

Better In The Shade

Imagine that it's going to be 90 degrees outside every day for a week! Your family is at the campground looking for *just* the right spot. Dad says, "Let's find a shady site!"
[Victor's family is much more comfortable in the hot sun than people are!]

It is *much* cooler in the shade of a tree, building, or beach umbrella. Being in the shade while playing or working puts us in a better mood and gives us more energy!
David and Moses, from the Bible, were shepherds. Imagine how hot it was for *them* when their sheep were in the sun all day! That is one reason they shared this treasure talk for today: *God is like shade*. With Him we feel rested and happy. **A**
God sent Jesus to save us from our sins *and* He rescues us from *many* of the troubles that visit us once in a while. **B, C** Ahhh, *that's* cool!

Treasure Talk: It is a HUGE help to trust God and find rest in Him--our Shade!

DIG DEEPER

A Ps. 91:1,2
B Mt. 11:28
C Ps. 121:5

Go in your backyard on a hot, sunny day. Just stand there for 3 minutes. Now stand under an umbrella or a leafy tree. Ah-h-h, feel better? That is just like our God . . . we feel better when we trust in Him!

Hope Rope

Rope has been used for thousands of years! Rope is used to lift, drag, and hold. It is used in climbing, boating, and building. Even Victor depends on rope to hold heavy loads on his back or to lead him over rough ground. When the *Bible* talks about rope it is treasure talk for *strength*!

The strongest type of rope is made of three cords braided together. Even Solomon, a very wise man in the Bible, said "A rope that has three parts wrapped together is hard to break."

There are three treasures wrapped up in this mystery rope language!

#1 Earlier you learned that God is three persons in one—Father, Son, and Holy Spirit (remember the apple?). They have different jobs, but "braided together" Father, Son, and Holy Spirit are one strong, perfect God!

#2 "Three" must be one of God's favorite numbers:

   He talks about Faith, Hope, and Love in the same sentence. B

   Jonah spent 3 days inside a big fish! C

   Jesus spent 3 days in a grave before He arose! D

#3 We need other people to keep us strong in following Jesus! E Family members and friends cheer us up, help us in trouble, and pray for us.

Treasure Talk: Just as a rope is strong enough to help or save, so is having God *and* friends He gives us.

A Ecc. 4:12
B 1 Cor. 13:13
C Jonah 1:17
D Mt. 12:40
E Prov. 12:26

Take one piece of ordinary string and just lay it on the table. Now braid *three* pieces of the same kind of string and lay *that* beside the single piece.
Which looks stronger? ☺

You Are The Apple of His Eye

Look long and carefully into eyes of a grown-up you love. What is at the very center? That dark, tiny circle is called the *pupil*. It's round. Victor's are football-shaped. God created the *pupil* to take in *light* so we can see. It's hard to see clearly in a dark room or outside at night because our eyes need *light* in order to see! *The pupil is the treasure of the eye!* We need it. We take care of it by protecting it.

God takes care of us because He treasures us! He keeps His eyes on us because He loves us so much! **A** THAT is why He calls us the "apple of His eye!" **B**

Unless you're on the phone, it is almost impossible to say that you love someone without looking into their eyes! If we could see Jesus, we would see Him staring into our eyes and saying, "I love you!" Think about that every single day! **He loves you!**

Treasure Talk: God loves us so much that He calls us the "apple of His eye!"

DIG DEEPER

A 1 Pet. 3:12
B Deut. 32:10

Apples are one of the few fruits that can really shine! Find one. With a clean, soft cloth, gently rub it until it glows! Stand back and stare at it. Say, "You're special to me!" THAT IS **EXACTLY** WHAT GOD SAYS ABOUT **YOU** ALL DAY, EVERY DAY!

Guard It

Victor knows all about "guarding." Donkeys are famous for being great protectors of sheep.

Presidents, prime ministers, kings, and queens live in houses, castles, or palaces that are very carefully protected. There are *guards* standing at the doors to make sure that only the invited people come in.

In the Bible, David the shepherd must have had trouble with what came out of his mouth once in a while (just like us)! He asked God to put a *guard* over his mouth and to put a *door* on his lips. **A**

By now you know that he didn't mean a *real* guard with a uniform or a *real* door! It's treasure talk for "Lord, help me to be very careful about what comes out of my mouth!"

If we ask God to help us with that, He will! He loves it when we ask! It means that we want to please Him. We *want* to say what is right and to speak kindly. If our minds have bad thoughts, we do *not* want them to slip out between our teeth and pass our lips. *We need guards!* **B**

Treasure Talk: Just like David, ask God to guard your mouth from saying bad or unkind words.

A Ps. 141:3
B Prov. 4:23

Make a deal with a friend, brother, or sister to help each other guard your lips! Maybe your new club could be called "God's Guard Donkeys" ☺

Cling Tightly

When you cross a busy street or you're in a crowded store with Mom or Dad, they will often say, "Hold my hand!" That's because they love you and they do not want you to wander away, get lost, or get hurt.

When God speaks about "hanging onto Him," He uses the word "cling." "Cling" is hanging on so tightly that there is *no way* of falling off or letting go!

Monkeys cling tightly to a tree they are climbing. Some flowers and vegetables cling tightly to poles or garden screens to grow straight up toward the sun.

Moses and Joshua, two great leaders in the Bible, told people to cling to God.  A, B

If we think, say, and do what God says is right, then we are clinging to Him!
We never want to let go!

We can't REALLY hold onto God's Hand until we get to heaven, but it is picture-perfect treasure talk to help us understand what *clinging* to Him means. C

Treasure Talk: Hang on to God. Trust Him. He will *never* let you go!

A Deut. 10:20
B Joshua 23:8
C Ps. 63:8

Find a favorite toy. Hold it very tightly and just for fun say, "Mine!"
That's what God says about you if you hold on to Him tightly...
"Mine! _____ is all Mine!"
(your name here)

Shine Like Stars

Perhaps, like Victor, you love being outside at night in the summer. When it is clear and cloudless, the night sky lights up with stars. It seems that they wink at us.

The sun is even a star! It just happens to be *closer* to us than the rest so it appears bigger. Stars will not burn out like a light bulb will.

Jesus calls Himself the "Light of the world." 🛠A People who do not know or love Jesus are living in the "*dark*"—remember *that* treasure talk?

You may have heard about a brave man named Daniel in the Bible. He was thrown into a lion's den because he prayed to God three times a day.

But God closed the lions' mouths! 🛠B

God later told His friend, Daniel, that if *any* of us tell other people about Jesus—how to love Him and live for Him—we will shine like stars forever and ever*!* 🛠C How amazing is that?

Our great God Who sent Light into the world (Jesus!) and Who created the sun, moon, and stars in the first place, gives us this bright treasure promise: we will be like light that never goes out if we tell others about Him! 🛠D

Treasure Talk: We will be like shining stars if we do what is right and tell our friends about Jesus!

A John 8:12
B Dan. 6:22
C Dan. 12:3
D Phil. 2:15

Sing or listen to the song, "This Little Light Of Mine." Shout out this part—"Don't let Satan blow it out; I'm going to let it shine!"

37

A Mirror Is Just A Mirror

Have you ever looked into a cracked or cloudy mirror? You have to squint your eyes and get really close just to see your face!

Paul, the amazing missionary who wrote at least 13 books of the Bible, tells us that we can't know *everything* about God and about heaven while we are here on this earth. There is sin here! The Bible's mystery language helps us understand that sin messes up how well we can know Jesus and God. We love Him like crazy, but knowing *everything* about Him is like looking at a dark, foggy mirror. A

But then, Paul gives us the **great news** that when we go to Heaven we will *see* Jesus Face-to-face! B No longer will we *wonder* what Jesus and God are like! No longer will we *wonder* what heaven is like. **Our wonders turn to WOW!**

Treasure Talk: Keep learning about God! Think about Him! Wonder about Him! Then in Heaven someday you will say, "Oh, Jesus, I've been waiting to meet You Face-to-face!" Get ready for the biggest HUG you've ever received! C

A 1 Cor. 13:12a
B 1 Cor. 13:12b
C Rev. 22:3-4

With permission, buy a cheap mirror at a dollar store. Ask Mom if she has some old lipstick you could use. Then write on the mirror: "Later, Alligator! I get to see Jesus Face-to-face someday! WOW!"

The Well That's Always Full

If you live in the country you may get your water from a deep well. There are pipes underground that bring that water into your sink or bathtub. You just have to turn on the facet, and boom—the water is there!

When the Bible was written, people had wells too, but they didn't have the pipes. They had buckets. The bucket was tied to a rope. Someone would let down the rope, scoop the water with the bucket, and bring it up. It was hard work! If it didn't rain for a while, the well could even go dry. People (and Victor) would be *very* disappointed and *very* thirsty.

In the Bible, Isaiah said that God's goodness and His help *never* run out. A

That's treasure talk for saying God ALWAYS has enough for us! The well of our salvation—**God**—is *always* full. He *always* has enough of whatever we need!

How has God helped *you*? What answers to prayer have *you* had? *Share them.* Tell a bunch of people. That's like pulling up the full bucket and sharing it. God's well is deep and full to overflowing. B

Treasure Talk: God's help, love, power, and goodness, NEVER run out! It's up to us to "spill it" with our mouths.

A Is. 12:2-3
B Ps. 71:14-16

How excited are you to tell a friend about a new pet, a new bike, a fun trip, a tooth that just came out? Be even MORE excited to tell them what God has done for you! Do it without fear! Be brave! It's God we are trying to please, not people!

Creation Treasures

When you hear the words, "sky," "mountains," or "ocean," your mind gets a picture in it of something far away, big and tall, or very deep. All three of those beauties were created by God! Our small, human brains cannot even *imagine* how far away the sky is, how high mountains really are, or how deep the ocean is.

When David the shepherd wrote Psalm 36, he couldn't look up those facts on a computer or in a book. He was probably laying on his back looking at the beauty above him and said something like this: "Your love, God, feels like it reaches to the sky—
SO BIG! And Your goodness, God, feels much taller than *any* mountain! And, God, Your decisions are so good and right that they feel deeper than the sea!" Then David, who must have been beside a peaceful river, added this: "Your love, Lord, is not only HUGE, it is also a *treasure.* Your gifts are like a tasty feast and every smile You give us is like a refreshing drink from Your river of joy."

Treasure Talk: Whenever we look up into the sky, see a tall mountain, look at an ocean, feast on great food, sit by a river, or think about real treasure, then we are *beginning* to know what a GREAT, BIG, LOVING, GOOD, AND AMAZING GOD WE HAVE! It's hard to describe!

DIG DEEPER Ps. 36:5-8

Take time to draw some mountains, sky, ocean, a river, and a treasure chest. Across the top or at the bottom write: Psalm 36:5–8. Share your picture with someone and tell them what Psalm 36 says!

Our Lion; Our King!

When we (or Victor) think about lions, we think about big, strong, powerful, protective animal leaders. They are *not* afraid of other animals, but they *do* have an enemy—the hyena.

In the very last book of the Bible, God's Treasure says that Jesus is like a lion. A

How can Jesus be like a lion AND like a lamb? Because He's God! THAT's why. He's gentle and loving as a lamb, yet powerful and mighty like a lion.

The hyena is a lion's enemy; Satan is our enemy. BUT we have the Bible and we know *this* is true:

BECAUSE JESUS DIED ON A CROSS FOR US,

GOD WINS THE BATTLE OVER SATAN! B

God is *so* much greater! C **Be jump-up-and-down happy right now!**

Treasure Talk: a lion is called "King of the Jungle." Jesus is the King of the World!

A Rev. 5:5
B Heb. 2:14
C 1 Jn. 1:4

ROAR this like a lion might if it could talk like you: "Jesus is like a lion and Satan loses <u>every</u> battle when he tries to get me to do wrong!" YAHOO!

41

God's Special Rain

Whether your family has a tiny garden *or* huge fields of corn, wheat, and soybeans, you still have to follow the right plan to get the crops to grow. The Bible's treasure today matches how *real* plants grow to how WE grow as Jesus' followers:

Step #1--Plow or rake the soil   >   Pray & read or listen to the Bible—God's words.

Step #2--Plant the seeds   >   Do what is right & good; obey God and your parents.

Step #3—Let the rain come   >   God's saving power because of Jesus Who died for you!

Step #4—Harvest   >   Your choices will be right AND you will live in heaven with God someday!

Gardeners and farmers would *never* refuse rain. Plants need it! WE NEED GOD!

Treasure Talk: Just as rain helps plants grow, God sends us His power and His love to help us grow.

DIG DEEPER   Hos. 10:12

With help and permission grow two twin plants from seed. Water both until they start popping out of the soil. Now stop watering one of them. How long is it before the dry one droops?

DON'T BE A DROOPY CHRISTIAN! WATER YOUR HEART AND LIFE WITH GOD!

Wheat or Weeds?

Jesus often told his friends *stories* to help them understand the treasures of being a Christian. Jesus' stories are rich with treasure!

In one of those stories he said there was a field full of wheat. As the wheat grew, the farmer also noticed that *weeds* were growing right up with the wheat. He couldn't pull up all the weeds without the wheat being ruined, so he left them together. When it was time to harvest (pick) the wheat, the farmer could *easily* tell which was which. **A**

The "wheat" is like us who believe in God. The "weeds" are people who do *not* love God. Everyone grows and lives together on earth. BUT when Jesus comes back to take us to heaven, He will *easily* be able to tell who is who! The Bible says it's because we will shine like the sun, which is a star, remember? **B**

People who are like weeds will try their best to get *us* to be like a weed. Only Satan likes weedy people. So just put on your "armor" and say, "NO!" **C**

Treasure Talk: The world is full of people who love God (like wheat). It's also full of people who don't (like weeds). Only God can tell the difference and *He's the One* Who will bring us to heaven someday!

DIG DEEPER
A Mt. 13:24-30
B Mt. 13:43
C Eph. 6:10-11

Draw a HUGE circle—that's the world. Fill it up with beautiful golden lines to look like wheat. Now draw some ugly looking black lines to look like weeds. Across the top write:

_____ is like wheat!
(your name here)

Catch Your Thoughts

Imagine you are walking your dog. It breaks its leash and starts running away. You shout, "Get back here, Jersey!"

Or imagine a pile of fresh, tasty green peas on your dinner plate. One rolls away. You say with a grin, "Get back here, Sweet Pea!"

Perhaps your hat blows off on a windy day. Immediately you try to snatch it back or run after it.

The Bible's treasure talk says we must do the same thing with our *thoughts*. **A** If we catch ourselves thinking something that we *know* is wrong, we have to rope that thought, rub it out, and change it! The Bible even tells us what to change it into—thoughts that are true, good, right, and full of honor. These kinds of thoughts are pleasing to God. **B** Think also about Jesus Himself—Someone we cannot see with our brown, green, or blue eyes, but Someone we *can* see with the "eyes of our hearts." **C**

Treasure Talk: God knows every one of our thoughts! Take charge of them by making them *very* good!

DIG DEEPER

A 2 Cor. 10:5
B Phil. 4:8
C 2 Cor. 4:18

Put about 10 cotton balls on the floor or table. Ask Dad or Mom to blow them around. Try catching one! Pretend those are like thoughts you have. Keep "catching" the bad ones and turn them into good ones!

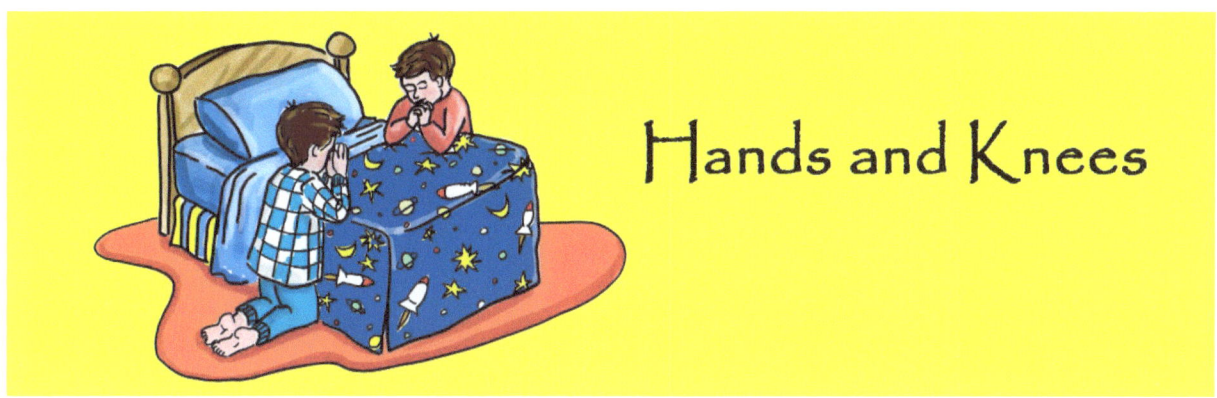

Hands and Knees

God created Victor with legs, knees, heels, and even elbows. He doesn't have hands; he has hooves. Knees bend and help Victor's and *your* body lift heavy loads. Our hands and Victor's hooves are very different. We have fingers and wrists that move in order to wave, write, wiggle, and work. And God, Who made us, gets *great* joy in seeing us fold our hands and bend our knees in prayer.

When the treasure talk in the Bible says to work at giving our hands and feet strength, **A** it means many things:

> Pray *more* with excitement and energy!
> Serve God with the work of your hands
> Help others stand strong in their "walk" with God. Cheer them on!

Our first prayer in the morning—kneeling and with folded hands—should be: "Lord, who needs me today? I want to give strength to THEIR hands and feet."

If you see a boy or girl in your school standing all alone at recess, YOU can be the hands and feet of Jesus by walking over to them and asking them to play with you. Not only will *you* feel like you're standing stronger, but they will too. And Jesus will be smiling! **B** **HE is the One we want to please.**

Treasure Talk: Make your hands and feet strong by working for Jesus to make the hands and feet of someone else strong too!

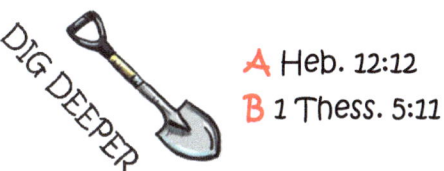

A Heb. 12:12
B 1 Thess. 5:11

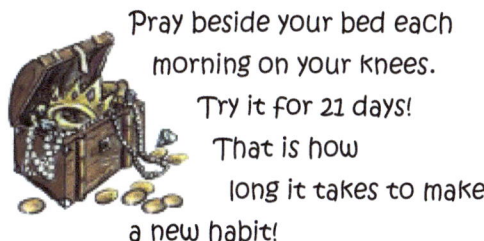

Pray beside your bed each morning on your knees. Try it for 21 days! That is how long it takes to make a new habit!

Be Like A Thirsty Deer

Have you ever been so thirsty that you shouted, "Help, I'm dyin'! I need water!"
Your parents or grandparents may say with a wink and a grin that you're acting like a "Drama Queen" or a "Drama King." Water is as close as the sink!

But imagine being Victor the donkey *or* a deer. They get thirsty too. Victor and his cousins go to a large water bowl that the farmer provides. But deer have to *search* for water in a river or lake. They will die without it.

A shepherd in the Bible saw *many* deer while watching sheep. When deer went running toward water, this thought-treasure came to his mind: *I want to be in that big of a hurry for God!* 🗲 **A, B** Is that what <u>you</u> want?

Sometimes you can hardly wait for a special gift or a special trip. God wants us to be *just* as excited for *Him*—even more excited!

How do you get that excitement? Think about ALL God has done for you and pray more—talk with Him often. Ask Him to make you more "thirsty" for Him. *He will!* 🗲 **C**

Treasure Talk: *Want God!* Want Him more than wanting a glass of cold water on a hot day.

DIG DEEPER
A Ps. 42:1,2
B Ps. 63:1
C Ps. 143:6

Make a list with words or pictures of EVERYTHING God has done for you and your family. Imagine Him saying, "Are you thirsty for even more? It's yours! Just be thirsty for Me!"

Are You A Victor?

That sounds like a crazy question! Of course you are not a donkey!

Victor has helped us dig and discover hidden treasures that are "buried" in the Bible. So, as we end this book it is important to know that even Victor's *name* has hidden meaning. It's *packed* with treasure! When someone wins a game, race, or contest, we say that they are the *winner!* Winner means "*victor.*" A *victor* gets a special prize—a ribbon, a badge, a crown, or a fancy piece of paper—that *proves* they've won.

YOU are a *victor* in God's eyes
- if you have asked Jesus into your heart and life,
- if you are "thirsty" for Him,
- if you are a "branch" of His and are growing "roots" and "fruit,"
- if you want to be His special "pot;" His "sheep,"
- if you want more than anything to keep "Digging for Treasure" in the Bible,

THIS MEANS YOU HAVE <u>FAITH</u>—BELIEVING IN GOD WHOM YOU CANNOT SEE YET!

FAITH IN JESUS, GOD'S SON, MEANS VICTORY! YOU'VE WON!

THE PRIZE: A HOME IN HEAVEN! A, B, C, D

Treasure Talk: YOU are a VICTOR if you have faith in Jesus and believe that God sent Him to die for your sins!

A 1 John 5:4
B 2 Tim. 4:7
C 1 Cor. 15:57
D Ps. 118:14

The Bible tells us the words we will hear when we get to heaven:
"You did well. You are a good servant who can be trusted . . . Come and share my happiness with me."

To ask God to live in your heart forever,
Victor invites you to pray this prayer!

Dear God, I want You to live in my heart forever! I am very sorry for all that I do wrong. You call it sin, Lord, and I am sorry for those sins. I believe that You sent Jesus to die on a cross in order to pay for all my sins. I believe He is making a place for me in heaven. Thank you for loving me and for knocking at the door of my heart. Today I invite You in to stay forever! Help me please to read Your letter to us—the Bible—and wear Your armor every day to guard and protect my heart from Satan. In Jesus' Name, Amen.

Verses are from one of these:
The Message **(MSG)**
The International Children's Bible **(ICB)**
The New International Version **(NIV)**
The New Living Translation **(NLT)**
New King James Version **(NKJV)**
Amplified Bible **(AMP)**
Common English Bible **(CEB)**
Contemporary English Version **(CEV)**

Page 3, He's THE Stone; You're A Stone

A 1 Samuel 2:2 (ICB) "There is no one holy like the Lord. There is no God but you. There is no Rock like our God."

B 1 Peter 2:4-5 (ICB) "The Lord Jesus is the "stone" that lives. The people of the world did not want this stone. But he was the stone God chose. To God he was worth much. So come to him. You also are like living stones. Let yourselves be used to build a spiritual temple..."

Page 4, A Safe Fort

A Psalm 32:7 (CEV) "You are my hiding place! You protect me from trouble."

B Psalm 62:8 (ICB) "People, trust God all the time. Tell him all your problems. God is our protection."

C Psalm 18:2 (CEV) "You are my mighty rock, my fortress, my protector, the rock where I am safe, my shield, my powerful weapon, and my place of shelter."

D Genesis 16:13 (MSG) "She answered God…You're the God who sees me!'"

Page 5, Not Like Victor

A Psalm 32:9 (ICB) "So don't be like a horse or donkey. They don't understand. They must be led with bits and reins, or they will not come near you."

B Psalm 32:8 (ICB) "The Lord says, "I will make you wise. I will show you where to go. I will guide you and watch over you."

Page 6, Fall Into His Arms

A Deuteronomy 33:27 (ICB) "The everlasting God is your place of safety. His arms will hold you up forever. He will force your enemy out ahead of you. He will say, 'Destroy the enemy!'"

B Psalm 56:3-4 (ICB) "When I am afraid, I will trust you. I praise God for his word. I trust God. So I am not afraid."

Page 7, Give Us A Hand, Lord

A Exodus 14 (MSG) "When the king of Egypt was told that the people were gone, he and his servants changed their minds. They said, "What have we done, letting Israel, our slave labor, go free?" So he…got his army together. He took six hundred of his best chariots, with the rest of the Egyptian chariots and their drivers coming along.

God made Pharaoh king of Egypt stubborn, determined to chase the Israelites as they walked out on him without even looking back. The Egyptians gave chase and caught up with them… As Pharaoh approached, the Israelites looked up and saw them—Egyptians! Coming at them!

They were totally afraid. They cried out in terror to GOD. They told Moses,…'What have you done to us?…'

Moses spoke to the people: 'Don't be afraid. Stand firm and watch GOD do his work of salvation for you today. Take a good look at the Egyptians today for you're never going to see them again.

GOD will fight the battle for you…'

GOD said to Moses:…'Order them to get moving. Hold your staff high and stretch your hand out over the sea: Split the sea! The Israelites will walk through the sea on dry ground. Meanwhile I'll make sure the Egyptians keep up their stubborn chase—I'll use Pharaoh and his entire army, his chariots and horsemen, to put my Glory on display so that the Egyptians will realize that I am GOD'…
Then Moses stretched out his hand over the sea and GOD, with a terrific east wind all night long, made the sea go back. He made the sea dry ground. The seawaters split.

The Israelites walked through the sea on dry ground with the waters a wall to the right and to the left. The Egyptians came after them in full pursuit, every horse and chariot and driver of Pharaoh racing into the middle of the sea. It was now the morning watch. GOD looked down…on the Egyptian army and threw them into a panic. He clogged the wheels of their chariots; they were stuck in the mud.

The Egyptians said, 'Run from Israel! GOD is fighting on their side and against Egypt!'

GOD said to Moses, 'Stretch out your hand over the sea and the waters will come back over the Egyptians, over their chariots, over their horsemen.'

Moses stretched his hand out over the sea…the sea returned to its place as before…The waters returned, drowning the chariots and riders of Pharaoh's army that had chased after Israel into the sea. Not one of them survived.

But the Israelites walked right through the middle of the sea on dry ground, the waters forming a wall to the right and to the left. GOD delivered Israel that day from the…Egyptians. And Israel…realized the tremendous power that GOD brought against the Egyptians. The people were in reverent awe before GOD and trusted in GOD and his servant Moses."

B Psalm 136:4, 12-14 (MSG) "Thank the miracle-working God, *His love never quits…* Took Israel in hand with his powerful hand, *His love never quits* Split the Red Sea right in half, *His love never quits.* Led Israel right through the middle, *His love never quits.*"

Page 8, Are You Smelling Sweet?

A 2 Corinthians 2:15 (ICB) "We are the sweet smell of Christ among those who are being saved and among those who are being lost."

Page 9, Are Your Prayers Smelling Sweet?

A Psalm 141:2 (CEV) "Think of my prayer as sweet-smelling incense…"
B Deuteronomy 7:6 (MSG) "GOD, YOUR GOD, chose you out of all the people on earth for himself as a cherished personal treasure."

Page 10, Just Taste It!

A Psalm 34:8 (MSG) "Open your mouth and taste…how good GOD is. Blessed are you who run to him."

B 1 Peter 2:2-3 (CEB) "Instead, like a newborn baby, desire the pure milk of the word. Nourished by it, you will grow into salvation, since you have tasted that the Lord is good."
C Psalm 119:103 (CEB) "Your word is so pleasing to my taste buds—it's sweeter than honey in my mouth!"

Page 11, Be Hungry and Thirsty

A Matthew 5:6 (MSG) "You're blessed when you've worked up a good appetite for God. He's food and drink in the best meal you'll ever eat."
B Psalm 63:1 (MSG) "God—you're my God! I can't get enough of you! I've worked up such hunger and thirst for God…"

Page 12, Bread Wonder

A John 6:1-13 (ICB) "…Jesus went across Lake Galilee. Many people followed him because they saw the miracles he did to heal the sick. Jesus went up on a hill and there sat down with his followers…Jesus looked up and saw a large crowd coming toward him. He said to Philip, 'Where can we buy bread for all these people to eat?' (Jesus asked Philip this question to test him. Jesus already knew what he planned to do.)
…Another follower there was Andrew…Andrew said, 'Here is a boy with five loaves of barley bread and two little fish. But that is not enough for so many people.'
Jesus said, 'Tell the people to sit down.' This was a very grassy place. There were about 5,000 men who sat down there. Then Jesus took the loaves of bread. He thanked God for the bread and gave it to the people who were sitting there. He did the same with the fish. He gave them as much as they wanted.
They all had enough to eat. When they had finished, Jesus said to his followers, 'Gather the pieces of fish and bread that were not eaten. Don't waste anything.' So they gathered up the pieces that were left. They filled 12 large baskets with the pieces that were left of the five barley loaves."
B John 6:33 (ICB) "God's bread is the One who comes down from heaven and gives life to the world."
C John 6:35 (ICB) "Then Jesus said, 'I am the bread that gives life.'"
D 1 Peter 1:3-4 (ICB) "Praise be to the God and Father of our Lord Jesus Christ. God has great mercy, and because of his mercy he gave us a new life. He gave us a living hope because Jesus Christ rose from death. Now we hope for the blessings God has for his children. These blessings are kept for you in heaven. They cannot be destroyed or be spoiled or lose their beauty."

Page 13, Lamb of God

A John 3:16 (ICB) "For God loved the world so much that he gave his only Son. God gave his Son so that whoever believes in him may not be lost, but have eternal life."
B John 1:29 (ICB) "The next day John saw Jesus coming toward him. John said, 'Look, the Lamb of God. He takes away the sins of the world!'"

Page 14, Go Fishing

A Luke 5:4-8 (ICB) "When Jesus had finished speaking, he said to Simon, 'Take the boat into deep water. If you will put your nets in the water, you will catch some fish.'
Simon answered, 'Master, we worked hard all night trying to catch fish, but we caught nothing. But you say to put the nets in the water; so I will.' The fishermen did as Jesus told them. And they caught so many fish that the nets began to break. They called to their friends

in the other boat to come and help them. The friends came, and both boats were filled so full that they were almost sinking. The fishermen were all amazed at the many fish they caught."
B Luke 5:10 (CEB) "Jesus said…'Don't be afraid. From now on, you will be fishing for people.'"
C Matthew 28:18-20 (ICB) "Then Jesus came to them and said… 'So go and make followers of all people in the world…Teach them to obey everything that I have told you. You can be sure that I will be with you always. I will continue with you until the end of the world.'"

Page 15, Are You In Rough And Deep Water?

A Mark 4:35-41(ICB) "That evening…the followers…went in the boat that Jesus was already sitting in…A very strong wind came up on the lake. The waves began coming over the sides and into the boat…Jesus stood up and commanded the wind and the waves to stop. He said, 'Quiet! Be still!' Then the wind stopped, and the lake became calm. Jesus said to his followers, 'Why are you afraid? Do you still have no faith?'"

B Matthew 14:22-33 (CEV) "Jesus made his disciples get into a boat and start back across the lake, but he stayed until he had sent the crowds away. Then he went up on a mountain where he could be alone and pray. Later that evening, he was still there.
By this time the boat was a long way from the shore. It was going against the wind and was being tossed around by the waves. A little while before morning, Jesus came walking on the water toward his disciples. When they saw him, they thought he was a ghost. They were terrified and started screaming.
At once, Jesus said to them, 'Don't worry! I am Jesus. Don't be afraid.'
Peter replied, 'Lord, if it is really you, tell me to come to you on the water.'
'Come on!' Jesus said. Peter then got out of the boat and started walking on the water toward him.
But when Peter saw how strong the wind was, he was afraid and started sinking. 'Save me, Lord!' he shouted. Right away, Jesus reached out his hand. He helped Peter up and said, 'You surely don't have much faith. Why do you doubt?'
When Jesus and Peter got into the boat, the wind died down. The men in the boat worshiped Jesus and said, 'You really are the Son of God!'"
C Isaiah 43:1-5 (MSG) "But now…'Don't be afraid, I've redeemed you. I've called your name. You're mine. When you're in over your head, I'll be there with you. When you're in rough waters, you will not go down. When you're between a rock and a hard place, it won't be a dead end—Because I am GOD, your personal God…your Savior. I paid a huge price for you…That's how much you mean to Me. *That's* how much I love you!...So don't be afraid: I'm with you…'"
D Isaiah 41:10 (ICB) "'So don't worry, because I am with you. Don't be afraid, because I am your God. I will make you strong and will help you. I will support you with my right hand that saves you.'"

Page 16, The Color Red

A Isaiah 1:18 (ICB) "The Lord says…'Your sins are red like deep red cloth…Your sins are bright red…'"
B Joshua 2:17-19 (ICB) "The men said to [Rahab], 'You must do as we say…You are using a red rope to help us escape. When we return to this land, you must tie it in the window through which you let us down. Bring your father, mother, brothers and all your family into your house. We can keep everyone safe who stays in this house.'"
C Exodus 12:7, 13 (ICB) "The people must take some of the [lamb's] blood. They must put it on the sides and tops of the doorframes…But the blood will be a sign on the houses where you are. When I see the blood, I will pass over you. Nothing terrible will hurt you when I punish the land of Egypt.'

Page 17, White As Snow

A Isaiah 1:18 (ICB) "Your sins are red like deep red cloth. But they can be as white as snow."
B Luke 15:10 (ICB) "…there is joy before the angels of God when one sinner changes his heart."
C Revelation 20:11 (NIV) "Then I saw a great white throne and him who was seated on it."

Page 18, Look At Jesus

A Hebrews 12:2 (ICB) "Let us look only to Jesus. He is the one who began our faith, and he makes our faith perfect. Jesus suffered death on the cross. But he accepted the shame of the cross as if it were nothing. He did this because of the joy that God put before him. And now he is sitting at the right side of God's throne."

Page 19, Earth Is God's Footstool

A Matthew 5:34,35 (CEV) "Heaven is God's throne…The earth is God's footstool…"
B Psalm 24:1 (CEV) "The earth and everything on it belong to the LORD. The world and its people belong to him."

Page 20, How's Your Me Power?

A Proverbs 25:28 (MSG) "A person without self-control is like a house with its doors and windows knocked out."
B 1 Peter 5:8 (ICB) "Control yourselves and be careful! The devil is your enemy. And he goes around like a roaring lion…"
C Psalm 60:10-12 (ICB) "God…Help us fight the enemy. Human help is useless. But we can win with God's help. He will defeat our enemies."

Page 21, A Strong, Safe Tower

A Proverbs 18:10 (ICB) "The Lord is like a strong tower where his people can run for safety."
B Psalm 27:5 (NIV) "For in the day of trouble he will keep me safe…"
C Joel 2:32 (CEB) "But everyone who calls on the Lord's name will be saved…"

Page 22, All Kinds of "Pots"

2 Corinthians 4:6-7 (ICB) "God once said, 'Let the light shine out of the darkness!' And this is the same God who made his light shine in our hearts. He gave us light by letting us know the glory of God that is in the face of Christ. We have this treasure from God. But we are only like clay jars that hold the treasure. This shows that this great power is from God, not from us."

Page 23, Weary, Worried, Or On Wings?

A Isaiah 40:28-31 (CEV) "Don't you know? Haven't you heard? The LORD is the eternal God, Creator of the earth. He never gets weary or tired; his wisdom cannot be measured. The LORD gives strength to those who are weary. Even young people get tired, then stumble and fall. But those who trust the LORD will find new strength. They will be strong like eagles soaring upward on wings; they will walk and run without getting tired."
B Psalm 27:14 (ICB) "Wait for the Lord's help. Be strong and brave and wait for the Lord's help."

Page 24, You Are A Temple

A Acts 2:32-33 (CEV) "All of us can tell you that God has raised Jesus to life! …and he was given the Holy Spirit, just as the Father had promised. Jesus is also the one who has given the Spirit to us…"
B Acts 17:24 (CEV) "This God made the world and everything in it. He is Lord of heaven and earth, and he doesn't live in temples built by human hands."
C 1 Corinthians 3:16 (ICB) "You should know that you yourselves are God's temple. God's Spirit lives in you."

Page 25, How Do People Read You?

A 2 Corinthians 3:3 (CEV) "You are like a letter written by Christ…"
B Proverbs 20:11 (CEV) "The good or bad that children do shows what they are like."
C Ephesians 4:29 (ICB) "When you talk, do not say harmful things. But say what people need—words that will help others become stronger. Then what you say will help those who listen to you."

Page 26, Part Of Christ's Body

A 1 Corinthians 12:27 (CEV) "Together you are the body of Christ. Each one of you is part of his body."
B Colossians 1:18 (ICB) "He is the head of the body…Everything comes from him. And he is the first one who was raised from death. So in all things Jesus is most important."

Page 27, Hear That Knock At The Door?

A Revelation 3:20 (CEV) "Listen! I am standing and knocking at your door. If you hear my voice and open the door, I will come in and we will eat together."
B John 3:16 (ICB) "For God loved the world so much that he gave his only Son. God gave his Son so that whoever believes in him may not be lost, but have eternal life."

Page 28, The Only Way To Heaven

A Matthew 7:13-14 (ICB) "Enter through the narrow gate. The road that leads to hell is a very easy road. And the gate to hell is very wide. Many people enter through that gate. But the gate that opens the way to true life is very small. And the road to true life is very hard. Only a few people find that road."
B John 14:6 (MSG) "Jesus said, 'I am the Road, also the Truth, also the Life. No one gets to the Father apart from me…'"
C John 16:33 (ICB) "In this world you will have trouble. But be brave! I have defeated the world!"

Page 29, You Are THE Salt

A Matt. 5:13 (CEV) "You are like salt for everyone on earth. But if salt no longer tastes like salt, how can it make food salty? All it is good for is to be thrown out and walked on."
B Mark 9:50 (CEV) "Salt is good. But if it no longer tastes like salt, how can it be made salty again? Have salt among you and live at peace with each other."

Page 30, An Instrument Doesn't Just Play Music

1 Peter 2:9-10 (MSG) "But you are the ones chosen by God, chosen for the high calling of priestly work, chosen to be a holy people, God's instruments to do his work and speak out for him, to tell others of the night-and-day difference he made for you—from nothing to something, from rejected to accepted."

Page 31, All Of Us Are Adopted

A Ephesians 1:5 (CEV) "God was kind and decided that Christ would choose us to be God's own adopted children."
B Romans 8:14-17 (CEB) "All who are led by God's Spirit are God's sons and daughters… but you received a Spirit that shows you are adopted as his children. With this Spirit, we cry, 'Abba, Father.' The same Spirit agrees with our spirit, that we are God's children. But if we are children, we are also heirs. We are God's heirs and fellow heirs with Christ…"

Page 32, Better In The Shade

A Psalm 91:1-2 (CEB) "Living in the Most High's shelter, camping in the Almighty's shade, I say to the LORD, 'You are my refuge, my stronghold! You are my God—the one I trust!'"
B Matthew 11:28 (CEB) "'Come to me, all you who are struggling hard and carrying heavy loads, and I will give you rest.'"
C Psalm 121:5 (ICB) "The Lord guards you. The Lord protects you as the shade protects you from the sun."

Page 33, Hope Rope

A Ecclesiastes 4:12 (ICB) "…A rope that has three parts wrapped together is hard to break."
B 1 Corinthians 13:13 (ICB) "So these three things continue forever: faith, hope and love…"
C Jonah 1:17 (ICB) "And the Lord caused a very big fish to swallow Jonah. Jonah was in the stomach of the fish three days and three nights."
D Matthew 12:40 (ICB) "Jonah was in the stomach of the big fish for three days and three nights. In the same way, the Son of Man will be in the grave three days and three nights."
E Proverbs 12:26 (NIV) "The righteous choose their friends carefully…"

Page 34, You Are The Apple Of His Eye

A 1 Peter 3:12 (CEB) "The Lord's eyes are on the righteous and his ears are open to their prayers."
B Deuteronomy 32:10 (MSG)" He threw his arms around [you], lavished attention on [you], guarding [you] as the apple of his eye."

Page 35, Guard It

A Psalm 141:3 (CEB) "Set a guard over my mouth, LORD; keep close watch over the door that is my lips."
B Proverbs 4:23 (NIV) "Above all else, guard your heart, for everything you do flows from it."

Page 36, Cling Tightly

A Deuteronomy 10:20 (CEB) "Revere the LORD your God, serve him, cling to him…"
B Joshua 23:8 (CEB) "Hold on to the LORD your God…exactly as you've done right up to today."

C Psalm 63:8 (CEB) "My whole being clings to you; your strong hand upholds me."

Page 37, Shine Like Stars

A John 8:12 (NIV) "'I am the light of the world. Whoever follows me will never walk in darkness, but will have the light of life.'"
B Daniel 6:22 (ICB) "'My God sent his angel to close the lions' mouths. They have not hurt me, because my God knows I am innocent.'"
C Daniel 12:3 (ICB) "'The wise people will shine like the brightness of the sky. Those who teach others to live right will shine like stars forever and ever.'"
D Philippians 2:15 (ICB) "Then you will be innocent and without anything wrong in you. You will be God's children without fault. But you are living with crooked and mean people all around you. Among them you shine like stars in the dark world."

Page 38, A Mirror Is Just A Mirror

A 1 Corinthians 13:12a (CEV) "Now all we can see of God is like a cloudy picture in a mirror."
B 1 Corinthians 13:12b (CEV) "Later we will see him face to face. We don't know everything, but then we will, just as God completely understands us."
C Revelation 22:3-4 (CEV) "[His] people will worship God and will see him face to face."

Page 39, A Well That's Always Full

A Isaiah 12:2-3 (MSG) "Yes, indeed—God is my salvation. I trust, I won't be afraid. GOD—yes GOD!—is my strength and song, best of all, my salvation! Joyfully you'll pull up buckets of water from the wells of salvation. And as you do it, you'll say, "Give thanks to GOD. Call out his name. Ask him anything! Shout to the nations, tell them what he's done, spread the news of his great reputation!'"
B Psalm 71:14-16 (CEV) "I will never give up hope or stop praising you. All day long I will tell the wonderful things you do…But you have done much more than I could possibly know. I will praise you, LORD God, for your mighty deeds and your power to save."

Page 40, Creation Treasures

Psalm 36:5-8 (CEV) "Your love is faithful, LORD, and even the clouds in the sky can depend on you. Your decisions are always fair. They are firm like mountains, deep like the sea…Your love is a treasure, and everyone finds shelter in the shadow of your wings. You give your guests a feast in your house, and you serve a tasty drink that flows like a river."

Page 41, Our Lion; Our King

A Revelation 5:5 (CEV) "…The one who is called both the 'Lion from the Tribe of Judah' and 'King David's Great Descendant' has won the victory."
B Hebrews 2:14 (ICB) "These children are people with physical bodies. So Jesus himself became like them and had the same experiences they have. He did this so that, by dying, he could destroy the one who has the power of death. That one is the devil."
C 1 John 1:4 (CEV) "Children, you belong to God, and you have defeated these enemies. God's Spirit is in you and is more powerful than the one that is in the world."

Page 42, God's Special Rain

Hosea 10:12 (CEV) "Plow your fields, scatter seeds of justice, and harvest faithfulness. Worship me, the LORD, and I will send my saving power down like rain."

Page 43, Wheat or Weeds?

A Matthew 13:24-30 (ICB) "Then Jesus told them another story. He said, 'The kingdom of heaven is like a man who planted good seed in his field...his enemy came and planted weeds among the wheat. Then the enemy went away. Later, the wheat grew...But at the same time the weeds also grew...The servants asked, "Do you want us to pull up the weeds?" The man answered, "No, because when you pull up the weeds, you might also pull up the wheat. Let the weeds and the wheat grow together until the harvest time. At harvest time I will tell the workers this: First gather the weeds and tie them together to be burned. Then gather the wheat and bring it to my barn."'"

B Matthew 13:43 (CEV) "But everyone who has done right will shine like the sun in their Father's kingdom. If you have ears, pay attention!"

C Ephesians 6:10-11 (CEV) "...let the mighty strength of the Lord make you strong. Put on all the armor that God gives, so you can defend yourself against the devil's tricks."

Page 44. Catch Your Thoughts

A 2 Corinthians 10:5 (ICB) "...capture every thought and make it give up and obey Christ."

B Philippians 4:8 (ICB) "...continue to think about the things that are good and worthy of praise. Think about the things that are true and honorable and right and pure and beautiful and respected."

C 2 Corinthians 4:18 (CEV) "Things that are seen don't last forever, but things that are not seen are eternal. That's why we keep our minds on the things that cannot be seen."

Page 45, Hands And Knees

A Hebrews 12:12 (CEB) "So strengthen your drooping hands and weak knees!"

B 1 Thessalonians 5:11 (NIV) "...encourage one another and build each other up..."

Page 46, Being Like A Thirsty Deer

A Psalm 42:1,2 (CEV) "As a deer gets thirsty for streams of water, I truly am thirsty for you, my God. In my heart, I am thirsty for you, the living God."

B Psalm 63:1 (CEB) "God! My God! It's you—I search for you! My whole being thirsts for you!"

C Psalm 143:6 (CEV) "Then I lift my hands in prayer, because my soul is a desert, thirsty for water from you."

Page 47, Are You A Victor?

A 1 John 5:4 (CEV) "Every child of God can defeat the world [Satan], and our faith is what gives us this victory."

B 2 Timothy 4:7 (CEB) "I have fought the good fight, finished the race, and kept the faith."

C 1 Corinthians 15:57 (ICB) "But we thank God! He gives us the victory through our Lord Jesus Christ."

D Psalm 118:14 (NLT) "The LORD is my strength and my song; he has given me victory."

E Matthew 25:23 (ICB) "The master answered, 'You did well. You are a good servant who can be trusted. You did well with small things...Come and share my happiness with me.'"

About the Author

Sharon Deur is a daughter of the King of kings and loves helping children know they are royalty too. She graduated from Calvin University with a degree in elementary education. She taught preschool, kindergarten, second, and fourth grades. She has led Bible Studies for adults and young Moms. She spent time mentoring for MOPS (Mothers of Preschoolers) and also training parents in how to implement Love and Logic ® techniques.

Pilgrim's Progress, which Sharon read as a young teen, gave her a profound appreciation for Biblical imagery. She and her magnificent husband live in Michigan. She is "Mom" to two phenomenal sons and two marvelous daughters-in-love. In her spare time, she loves to read, walk, bike, and kayak.

About the Illustrator

Deborah Smith's love for art was nurtured at a young age, and has developed into an award winning, internationally sold artist. Her focus is to honor God through her art. She has taken her love for Christ and her passion for art and incorporated them into her life's work as an illustrator, painter, sculptor, and art instructor.

Prior to her current vocation in book illustrating, she had a distinguished and prestigious career as a Walt Disney World Artist, Designer and Art Director. She has received many accolades and awards her art and continues to exhibit her work throughout the Central Florida area. Deborah resides in Orlando, Florida with her husband.

"It truly is a blessing to pursue and share my passion for art. I will never tire of the joy and fulfillment it brings."

www.deborahsmithfineart.com

www.3-deborah-smith.pixels.com